HOW TO CREATE
SUCCESSFUL
SPECIAL EDUCATION
TEAM MEETINGS

HOW TO CREATE SUCCESSFUL SPECIAL EDUCATION TEAM MEETINGS

A GUIDE FOR CASE MANAGERS

Techniques for engaging staff and parents to make your SPED meetings productive and positive

Robert Scobie, MA, PhD
Founder of Common Goal, LLC

Tell me, I may listen.
Teach me, I may remember.
Involve me, I will do it.

– CHINESE PROVERB

White River Press • Amherst, Massachusetts

How to Create Successful Special Education Team Meetings: A Guide for Case Managers

Book and cover design:
Douglas Lufkin, Lufkin Graphic Designs

White River Press
P.O. Box 3561
Amherst, MA 01004
www.whiteriverpress.com

ISBN: 978-1-887043-09-0

Library of Congress Cataloging-in-Publication Data

Scobie, Robert, 1936-
    How to create successful special education team meetings : a guide for case
    managers / by Robert Scobie, PhD, Founder of Common Goal, LLC.
    pages cm
    ISBN 978-1-887043-09-0 (pbk. : alk. paper)
1. Special education--United States--Management. 2. Educational leadership--United
States. I. Title.
LC3981.S39 2014
371.9--dc23
                              2014005424

TABLE OF CONTENTS

HOW TO CREATE
SUCCESSFUL
SPECIAL EDUCATION
TEAM MEETINGS

INTRODUCTION

During my 15 years as a special educator in elementary and secondary public schools, I witnessed the value of actively involving parents in their child's education by teaching parents to:

- share personal information to help the school staff get to know their child better;

- act as advocates for change if things were not going well for their child;

- demonstrate support and encouragement for their child while he or she worked at home on school assignments.

We know that when educators and parents work together to support learning, the children benefit. They achieve greater results in school, stay in school longer, and like school better.

Though federal special education (SPED) regulations require parents to be involved with their child's education, they provide little guidance on how to effectively engage them in the team process, especially with regard to both requisite and "as needed" meetings. The complexities of the SPED process often make parents uncertain about how to get actively involved; parents often question the value of their input. But because school team members and parents have different experiences and knowledge about the child, if they share their perspectives in constructive ways, they can help the child reach his or her potential and avoid misunderstandings throughout the process.

This guide contains proven strategies that my research and experience have found effective in facilitating SPED team meetings, and in ensuring that school professionals and parents collaborate in positive ways that will ultimately create the best educational experience for the child. It also contains templates to help you organize your meeting preparation, to help parents to create a "checklist" of concerns, and for you to record and keep track of the progress of active steps that will help implement the plan and simplify effective follow-up.

THE CASE OF TOM BRUNO

Imagine yourself as the Case Manager for Tom Bruno, a fictional fourth grader and special needs student with a learning disability in written expression and with behavioral issues that border on Attention Deficit Disorder.

In a conversation with his mother, you report that Tom continues to struggle to follow classroom rules. You also tell her he has shown little improvement either in writing or in self-management and social skills. Mrs. Bruno reveals that she has been having difficulty with Tom at home, especially in trying to get him to do his writing homework. She says that she and her husband would like you to call an Individual Education Plan (IEP) meeting to review Tom's writing program and to revise his behavior plan.

Preparing for team meetings takes time. We know, too, that involving parents in the preparation for a meeting presents a challenge. But bridging the gap between school and home, between professional educator and parent can lead to constructive collaboration. As the Case Manager, it is up to you to provide support for the parents and engage them in meetings that are meaningful and productive, and will result in a better organized, more streamlined meeting for all members of Tom's special education team.

Ultimately, this will lead to Tom enjoying the benefits of improved performance in school.

The material in this guide will show you how to create a successful special education meeting. It is organized into three parts:

1. Preparation for the meeting

2. Participation in the meeting

3. Follow-up to the meeting

Follow the guidelines and use the templates. If you have any questions or need more information, see my contact information at the end of this guide. I welcome any and all input about your experiences with this program.

– Robert Scobie

PART ONE: PREPARING FOR THE TEAM MEETING

Using the example of our case of Tom Bruno, let's say a one-hour team meeting has been scheduled on a Wednesday afternoon at Tom's school. As Tom's Case Manager, you will be the facilitator of the meeting. In addition to you, the expected participants will be:

- the school system's special education director
- the behavior specialist
- Tom's regular education teacher
- the school nurse
- the school counselor
- Tom's parents

The purpose of the meeting will be to review Tom's writing program and to revise his behavior plan. For the most successful outcome, well-organized preparation is essential, beginning with concrete steps to ensure that Tom's parents' goals are aligned with the objectives of the team of specialists.

DETERMINE TOM'S PRESENT LEVEL OF PERFORMANCE

The first step toward meeting preparation is to collect data on and write down Tom's present level of performance in school relative to his IEP goals and objectives, including:

- academic skills

- grades

- problem-solving skills

- interpersonal skills

- motor skills

- decision-making skills

- communication skills

- organizational skills

- progress in general curriculum

- rate by which a task is accomplished

- amount of supervision/direction required

- amount of time sustained at task

- task completion

- quality of work

- number of steps in a series that student can complete

STEP 2:

MEET THE PARENTS

Meet with parents in their home (if possible) to ask about their concerns and personal goals about the upcoming meeting. This will enable you to set their agenda for the meeting and will help you build a closer relationship with them. During your meeting with the parents, you should:

1. Share the staff's concerns about Tom's present level of performance and their views on his strengths. Explain to them that based on observations and conferences with Tom's teacher and providers, you have determined the following:

   Academic/Educational Achievement and Learning Characteristics (current levels of knowledge and development in subject and skill areas, expected rate of progress in acquiring skills, and information and learning style):

   STRENGTHS: Reading skills on grade level; learns best when materials are presented visually; responds appropriately when reminded; enjoys books about nature and animals with pictures like those in the National Geographic books; works well one-on-one with teacher; will offer help to other students if asked; wants adult approval.

   WEAKNESSES: Testing and classroom assignments indicate written expression difficulties including:

   • Omits punctuation, spells poorly, and does not sequence sentences in a logical order in written work (topic sentence, supporting sentences, conclusion).

- Lacks motivation to write even on topics of interest.

- Written expression difficulties result in a slower pace of progress (it takes Tom, on average, twice as long as his peers to complete an assignment, which makes it difficult for him to complete tests requiring written expression within a prescribed time period).

- Has difficulty taking notes in class and understanding and benefiting from notes taken.

- When working on his own at his desk, he spends much of his time staring out the window or looking at what other students are doing.

ORGANIZATIONAL SKILLS: relies on following the actions of his peers. Can follow directions with up to 3-steps from teacher independently.

MEMORY/ATTENTION: has difficulty remembering homework assignments and what books to bring to class.

SOCIAL DEVELOPMENT (this encompasses the degree and quality of the student's relationships with peers and adults, his or her feelings about self, and social adjustment to school and community environments):

- When engaged in a group activity, Tom acts in a controlling way, speaking loudly, grabbing needed materials from other students, and doing things the way that he wants and in his own way. Most other students still avoid having anything to do with him, leaving him virtually friendless.

- His one close friend, whom Tom tends to follow, is a very active and distracting child who frequently misbehaves (e.g. plays noisily with objects at his desk, leaves his seat frequently for things like getting a drink of water, sharpening his pencil, going to the bathroom, etc.).

- Tom needs to work on acquiring the social and work skills that will enable him to get along with fellow students and respond appropriately to supervision.

2. Learn what the parents' specific goals will be for the team meeting; fill out an Agenda form (on page 14).

3. Discuss how the concerns of parents and staff can provide a common focus for problem solving.

4. Help parents see themselves as partners with staff in creating an effective writing and behavior plan for Tom.

5. Provide ideas about how to participate constructively in the meeting.

6. Notify the parents that they will receive a "Notice of Meeting."

Prior to a team meeting, contact with parents is essential:
- **By phone, e-mail, or, preferably, in person.**
- **Meet in the parents' home or at school if the student is a new referral or if the issue is big.**

ALIGN PARENTS' GOALS WITH TEAM MEETING OBJECTIVES.

When you meet with the parents, it will be important to document their goals to align them with the team objectives. For parents to engage actively in the team meeting, they must feel that the staff is acknowledging their needs and interests for their child. When parents feel valued by staff team members they have a greater sense of belonging to the group.

In our example, you ask Tom's mother if she and her husband would meet with you at their home to discuss their concerns and plan for the team meeting. This is a chance to develop a closer relationship with them and to help them clarify their goals and priorities. She agrees.

During the home visit, empathize with their frustrations with Tom at home. Share your own thoughts about Tom's behavior in the classroom and provide more in-depth information about the school's efforts to help Tom with both his writing and behavior management. You feel that if he could apply strategies that would help him focus, he would be better even at writing.

To prepare for the Team Meeting, use an Agenda form (found on page 14) to help the family prioritize their concerns and determine what they hope to get out of the team meeting. This provides you with the chance to discuss and clarify not only relevant items, but also ideas as to how they might participate with regard to each item. In addition, you:

- Encourage both parents to be open with the team about their concerns and to view the team as partners in problem-solving Tom's writing and behavior plan.

- Mention that the team meeting will provide an opportunity for the whole team to generate alternative ideas about how to work with Tom both in school and at home.

- Tell the parents that you have asked the school's behavior specialist to attend the team meeting to help the team review and revise Tom's behavior plan.

> **It is essential to identify agenda items for the team meeting with the parents to ensure that their concerns are included.**

STEP 4:
SET THE TEAM MEETING AGENDA & RULES

By photocopying the template for the Agenda form on page 14, you will help parents organize their thoughts about how the team meeting might address their concerns. In addition, you should post the completed Agenda for all team members to see before the start of the meeting. Segments of the Agenda form include:

ITEM: Write a title for each item or topic that needs to be considered. Use one line (or box) per item.

DESIRED OUTCOME: Insert the result you would like to have for each topic. This is perhaps the most important step in agenda planning.

PRIORITY: Identify high priority items. Rank the items in order, noting that those not covered in the meeting can be addressed at the next meeting.

TIME: Project the amount of time you will need to discuss each topic and achieve a desired outcome. Without planning, it is easy to underestimate how much time will be needed to discuss all topics during the entire meeting.

WHO: Assign the name of the person who will be responsible for seeing the topic through to completion.

HOW: This relates to the process for dealing with the topic. Do team members need to engage in a dialogue or a discussion; do they need to brainstorm alternatives or reach a consensus; should they be given feedback, etc.?

TASK COMPLETED: After the person responsible for each topic has addressed and completed the task, insert the staff's initials and date here for future reference.

Using our example of Tom Bruno, see the next page for how the Agenda for the team meeting should look:

You will find a blank agenda template on the following page. Make a photocopy of this template and fill it out prior to each team meeting. Completing the form validates the goals and gives each parent and team member a clear voice in deciding how they can be achieved. (If you enlarge it by 122% while photocopying, the form will fill an 8.5 x 11 sheet.)

ITEM	DESIRED OUTCOME	PRIORITY	TIME	WHO	HOW	TASK COMPLETED
Tom's behavior	Identify probs./ success	High	15 mins.	Case Mgr.	Dialogue/Discuss	
Behavior plan	Change-address problems	High	15 mins.	Behav. Spec.	Present./Discuss	
Writing problems	Identify difficulties	High	10 mins.	Case Mgr.	Present./Discuss	
Writing progress	Modify to motivate Tom	High	10 mins.	Teacher	Discussion	

13

ITEM	DESIRED OUTCOME	PRIORITY	TIME	WHO	HOW	TASK COMPLETED

STEP 5:

ALIGN STAFF GOALS WITH TEAM MEETING OBJECTIVES

After having met with the parents, but prior to the team meeting, you should contact all staff members who will be participating and take the following steps:

1. Ask each staff member for his or her priority for the team meeting.

2. Determine his or her expected outcome for the team meeting.

3. Share the parents' (in our example, the Brunos) concerns about their son's behavior and their questions about the adequacy of the existing behavior plan. Stress the importance of the parents as partners.

4. Share the agenda worked out by the parents. Ask if any other items (or topics) need to be added to the list.

5. Determine if any of the agenda items can be handled outside of the team meeting.

6. Clarify normative expectations for the meeting. Legitimize the role of "devil's advocate" in the event that the team has difficulty generating alternative ideas.

7. Discuss ideas about strategies that might be used relative to the agenda items.

After completing the seven steps above, you learned that while the staff agreed that all agenda items should be included, they wanted to address the relationship between Tom's behavior and his writing difficulties as a single topic, rather than two, as indicated in the proposed agenda. They felt that the discussion could encompass both items together, which would also save time. You shared their concerns about time and said you would think about how to modify the agenda. As Case Manager, it is your decision to screen the agenda items to be presented to the Team at the start for their acceptance or change.

A diagram of the agenda-building process follows.

> **Prior to the team meeting, it is essential to work with each staff team member to:**
> - **Share parents' concerns and their agenda**
> - **Stress that parents are partners on the team**
> - **Ask for their input about the student's present level of behavior and academic performance relative to his IEP goals and objectives**
> - **Ask if any of their concerns could be dealt with outside of the team meeting**
> - **Set the stage for problem-solving**

THINGS TO REMEMBER:

- **DETERMINE NORMATIVE EXPECTATIONS**

Normative expectations – "norms" – represent shared expectations about what is appropriate and acceptable behavior in the group: what is okay to do, and what is not okay to do, in specific situations.

Norms, as rules of behavior for group members, are not usually made public, but have a strong influence over members' behavior and contribute to the stability of the group. When a team's expectations are clear and members meet (or exceed) expectations, trust and an increased sense of belonging are natural byproducts.

In planning for the team meeting, you should be particularly eager to clarify normative expectations with staff for two reasons:

- Some members might be reticent about expressing different views regarding a student's behavior (such as Tom's in our example). Agreeing publicly to norms that support openness and problem solving is important; you should emphasize the role of "devil's advocate" as a way to generate alternative views.

- As facilitator, you are expected to manage the flow of the team meeting which means keeping the team on topic, insuring that members listen to each other, making sure the parents' views are respected, asking clarifying and probing questions, and monitoring the time. You want to be able to manage who talks to whom about what and how without unfairly dismissing a member who might want to speak.

Teams don't need a lot of ground rules to work together well, but everyone on the team should agree to them and share responsibility for ensuring that they are followed.

- **SET THE GROUND RULES**

    Ask the staff the following questions about ground rules regarding how team members should communicate DURING the team meeting:

    - Are interruptions acceptable?

    - Should you call on a team member before he or she speaks?

    - What about side conversations?

- Will it be all right to question an authority figure's view?

- If during dialogue, one or more team members make a judgment about someone else's idea, should you stop the action and remind participants to be nonjudgmental?

- What constitutes respectful behavior towards other team members?

Once the ground rules are determined, you should write them on a flip chart prior to the meeting so the team can review and, hopefully, accept them. If accepted, the team can move quickly into the main part of the meeting.

- **TEAM MEETING STRATEGIES**

By reviewing agenda items with the staff, you have the chance to share possible strategies you might use, including:

- Asking clarifying and probing questions

- Paraphrasing for understanding

- Seeking more detailed information

- Checking for other's feelings

- Describing behaviors adversely affecting the team

You especially want to set the stage for problem solving beforehand in order to legitimize open-ended questions such as:

- Ask: "Why?" Treat the other's view or position as an opportunity rather than an obstacle.

- Ask: "Why not?" If the other is reluctant to share his/her interests, propose an option and ask: "Why not do it this way?" or "What would be wrong with this approach?"

- Ask: "What if?" Introduce the other to a host of possible options. Brainstorm the alternatives and then ask: "What if?" about each one.

- Ask: "What if we don't?" Discuss what might happen if this is not done or not included in the plan.

- Ask: "How will the action satisfy your interests or resolve your concerns?"

Planning ahead will allow the team meeting to flow smoothly without unexpected surprises that could hamper progress.

PART TWO: CONDUCTING THE TEAM MEETING

As the facilitator of the team meeting, on the day of the meeting, review some basic, but important, points and strategies:

- Identify challenging behaviors that might occur.

- Know strategies to deal with challenging behaviors.

- Know how to create a climate of cooperation among team members.

- Prepare ways to enhance more active participation of the parents if they seem reticent to express their views.

- Plan to sit next to the parents to reinforce support for them.

- Prepare ways to insure that the dialogue/discussion stays on topic.

- Determine who will be timekeeper and the recorder and how notes will be recorded.

Once you have started the meeting, remember to be sensitive to the interpersonal communications that take place during both the dialogue and discussion (see below for distinction between dialogue and discussion). Be especially mindful of challenging behaviors that might have a negative effect. These include:

- Disregarding another's point of view.

- Changing the subject without explanation.

- Expressing certainty about the issues being discussed.

- Using technical terms that parents may not understand.

- Interrupting, cutting people off while they are talking.

- Polarizing, pushing people to take sides.

- Saying "Yes, but..." a lot, thus discounting the contributions of others.

- Personalizing issues and agenda topics: taking all remarks as directed toward persons rather than ideas.

- Directing behavior that focuses more at bolstering team morale at the expense of critical thinking.

- Believing that "silence means consent."

> **It is essential to be aware of challenging behaviors that could have a negative effect on the meeting and to respond in a constructive way.**

If any of the above behaviors occur, be prepared to exercise your authority as facilitator in a constructive way. Some responses you can be prepared to use are:

- Listen attentively; paraphrase to understand, not simply repeat, what the other said.

- Seek information to understand the speaker.

- Describe observable behaviors that influence the team and name the problem behavior.

- Directly report your own thoughts and feelings.

- Check to learn whether an individual's statement had the intended effect on other team members.

- Slow down the conversation by playing it back. For example, tell the other, "Let me just make sure I understand what you are saying;" then paraphrase the other speaker's statement.

- Ask problem-solving questions (refer to Team Meeting Strategies on pages 19-20).

- Ask for the other speaker's advice. For example, ask, "What would you suggest that we do?", or "What would you do if you were in (person's name) shoes?"

- Ask, "What makes that fair?" You may think the other's viewpoint or position is unreasonable, but instead of rejecting it, use it as a jumping-off point for a discussion about fairness. Assume that he or she thinks it is reasonable and say, "You must have good reasons for thinking that's a reasonable solution. I'd like to hear them."

In addition to being alert to challenging behaviors and preparing possible responses, you should be especially tuned in to how integral the Brunos feel on the team; if they are confused about any technical terms used; and whether or not what the team is discussing matches their personal goals and expectations for the meeting. In order to try to intuit how they are feeling, ask them periodically, "Are we addressing the questions and concerns that are important to you?" Remember that you will be sitting next to the Brunos to reinforce support for them.

Since the major task of the meeting is to review Tom's writing difficulties and possibly revise his behavior plan, your goal, as facilitator, is to create a climate of openness so that divergent ideas are encouraged and examined thoroughly. Below are "freeing responses" (with examples) that represent behaviors that can enhance openness that you can model and encourage other team members to demonstrate. The responses also tend to encourage parents to express their views.

FREEING RESPONSES

- Listen attentively; paraphrase to understand, not simply repeat, what the other has said.

    "Let me check out what I understood you to say."

- Check impressions of the other's feelings.

    "I hear some frustration behind your statement."

- Seek information to understand the other.

    "In order for me to understand your view, I need more information."

- Offer information that is relevant to the other's concern.

    "I'd like to add some information to what you've already given me."

- Describe observable behaviors that influence him or her.

    "It seems that you're very accepting when someone argues with you."

- Directly report his or her feelings.

  "I feel frustrated by your opinion."

- Offer your opinions or state your value position in an open way.

  "I think we can make the process more efficient."

DIALOGUE, DISCUSSION, & DECISION-MAKING

There are three important steps to implement during the team meeting: dialogue, discussion, and decision-making.

DIALOGUE refers to the "free flow of meaning between people" and is characterized by shared inquiry, nonjudgmental listening, and reflection. In our example, dialogue helps the team generate diverse ideas about the nature of Tom's problem. Unlike with brainstorming, dialogue helps team members build on the ideas of others by emphasizing less quantity and more exploration. Divergent ideas are encouraged.

DISCUSSION involves an exchange of views during which judgment plays a key role. The primary purpose of discussion is to have one's views accepted by the group. Discussion allows the team to critically examine each idea.

DECISION-MAKING lets the group evaluate the alternative ideas, select a preferred view, and reach a decision. This assessment of each idea will lead the team to decisions that pertain to the resolution of the problem(s).

As you think about the meeting, you wonder which agenda items can best be handled by "dialogue" and which by "discussion."

You think it might be good if the team engages in dialogue about the causes of Tom's continued struggles to follow classroom rules. The team doesn't seem to have a clear idea about these, and probing beneath the surface to reveal any underlying forces that affect his behavior is likely to be beneficial. As facilitator, it will be important for you to keep the dialogue moving. You can even be a participant by modeling dialogue. For example, after a member has expressed a particular view, you might say, "The opposite may also be true."

Sometimes team members become defensive during both the dialogue and discussion steps. Some might feel implicitly blamed if, for example, changes in program implementation are recommended over current practice. If that occurs, turn to the aforementioned "freeing responses" to help you handle team member defensiveness.

One useful strategy for getting at underlying causes of behavior is Force Field Description & Analysis (see below). As you think about using the Force Field technique regarding Tom, imagine the following forces that affect his academic work and behavior. (See the completed form on page 27.)

List the forces on the flip chart as the team raises them. This enables the team to discuss each and prioritize them. Examine each force with the intent to increase the positive forces and curb those that are blocking the student's movement toward the goal, thus, hopefully providing a basis for improvement – in Tom's case, improvement in both his behavior and writing skills.

Finally, be mindful of time to make sure the team doesn't get bogged down on one step at the expense of the others.

EXAMPLE FOR TOM BRUNO:
FORCE FIELD DESCRIPTION & ANALYSIS

Goal(s)

Tom needs to:

1) increase his self-management skills in order to control his aggressive and disruptive behavior;

2) work more constructively with others in a group;

3) sustain attention to the task during desk work;

4) show increased motivation to write about topics of interest.

Current Situation

FORCES FOR	FORCES AGAINST
Pro-Social/Academic Behaviors & Contexts	**Problem Behaviors & Contexts**
1. Wants adult approval	1. Peer rejection
2. Seeks out one-on-one time with teacher	2. One close friend; distracting
3. Offers help to other students	3. Isolates self from group
4. Avoids conflict if not his issue	4. Needs teacher more than others
5. Likes National Geographic books; likes to read	5. Follower
6. Can write in complete sentences	6. Problems when given choices
	7. Can't do independent desk work
	8. During group instruction, Tom doesn't understand directions for independent work
	9. Dislikes writing; no motivation; lacks skills

FORCE FIELD STEPS:

1. In the column under **FORCES FOR**, list the behaviors & contexts that enhance the student's movement toward the goal.

2. Under **FORCES AGAINST**, list behaviors & contexts which block the student from achieving the goal.

3. To analyze the Force Fields (e.g., behaviors & contexts), ask the following questions:

   - How clear are you about the behavior & contexts as a force?

   - How important is the behavior as a force? (E.g., the most important behavior is one that, if changed, would yield the greatest movement toward the goal.)

   - How easily can the behavior and contexts be changed?

4. Based on the Force Field Description & Analysis, develop an action plan for the student.

Make a photocopy of the template on the next page and fill it out with the child's appropriate behaviors and contexts. (If you enlarge it by 122% while photocopying, the form will fill an 8.5 x 11 sheet.) Use the example on page 27 as a guideline.

FORCE FIELD DESCRIPTION & ANALYSIS

Goal(s)

Current Situation

FORCES FOR

Pro-Social/Academic
Behaviors & Contexts

FORCES AGAINST

Problem Behaviors
& Contexts

PART THREE:
CLOSING AND FOLLOW-UP FOR THE TEAM MEETING

When closing the team meeting:

- Review actions and prioritize next steps.

- Check with parents to make sure they agree with any decisions that have been made. If they do, have them sign appropriate forms. If they do not, be sure they have additional time to express their response.

- Clarify what future changes to the plan can be made without another team meeting.

- Ask the parents what the best method for communicating with them is (e-mail, phone, written notes) and on what days and/or times.

To follow up the team meeting:

- Summarize the meeting minutes in writing. Place the pertinent decisions in boldface type or ALL CAPS. Share with parents.

- Make sure each teacher and provider is informed about who is responsible for implementing the team's decisions and the dates for completion.

- Set date for next meeting, if one will be necessary.

- Gather information from the team about how the meeting went.

- Discuss with Tom the changes that will be made. Develop with him a daily monitoring of his work; meet with him weekly to debrief him.

- Keep Tom's parents apprised of Tom's progress as necessary and appropriate.

- As tasks are completed, be sure to fill out the "Task Completed" column of your original Agenda Form.

It is essential to follow-up with the parents and ask if their personal goals were accomplished. Ask if they felt other members of the team were responsive to their needs, interests, and concerns. Follow-up with each teacher and provider on implementation of team decisions.

CONCLUSION

As a Case Manager, you have a responsibility to create positive communication between students, their parents or guardians, school professionals, and other members of the student's Special Education Team. By learning to create a successful SPED team meeting, your meetings will be more productive and satisfying to all parties. The student may be on your case list for years to come: study this book and use the tools. Everyone involved will benefit from the results.

A companion guide to this book has been written especially for parents: *How to be an Effective Participant in Special Education Team Meetings: A Guide for Parents*. *Ways for Parents to Actively Partner with Staff in SPED Team Meetings*. It is available at Amazon.com, Barnes & Noble, or at www.effectiveSPEDmeetings.com.

If you would like information on how to arrange for a meeting with Robert Scobie, contact him at bob@effectiveSPEDmeetings.com, or visit his website at www.effectiveSPEDmeetings.com.

CASE MANAGER CHECKLIST

BEFORE TEAM MEETING, MEET WITH PARENTS

- By phone, e-mail, or preferably, in person at their home or at the school

- Identify agenda items with them

- Reassure them that their concerns will be addressed

- Make sure they feel supported

BEFORE TEAM MEETING, TALK WITH EACH STAFF MEMBER

- Review parents' concerns

- Stress that parents are partners

- Obtain update of student's performance

- Ask for specific team meeting priorities

- Ask what can be addressed outside of the team meeting

- Set the stage for problem solving

PARTS OF A TEAM MEETING AGENDA

- Item or Topic
- Desired Outcome
- Priority
- Time
- Who
- How
- Task Completed

CHALLENGING BEHAVIORS THAT CAN NEGATIVELY AFFECT THE TEAM MEETING

- Disqualifying another's point of view
- Changing the subject without explanation
- Expressing certainty
- Using technical terms
- Interrupting
- Pushing people to take sides
- Saying "Yes, but..." a lot
- Personalizing issues and agenda topics
- Directing behavior that focuses on bolstering team morale
- Believing that "silence means consent"

CONSTRUCTIVE RESPONSES IN THE TEAM MEETING

- Listen attentively

- Paraphrase to understand

- Ask for more information

- Name problem behaviors that are influencing the team

- Report your own thoughts and feelings

- Check team members for intended effect of others' comments

- Slow down the conversation

- Ask problem-solving questions

- Ask for others' advice

- Ask "What makes that fair?"

RESOURCES

Among the references below, the author wishes to acknowledge his indebtedness to the following for their strategy ideas: Richard A. Schmuck, Philip J. Runkel, William Ury, and Peter M. Senge.

Barrett, Jon H., *Individual Goals and Organizational Objectives*, Ann Arbor, MI: Institute for Social Research, The University of Michigan, 1970, pp. 3, 11.

Beck, Stephenson J. & Keyton, Joann. "Perceiving Strategic Meeting Interaction," *Small Group Research*, Vol. 40, No. 2 (April, 2009), pp. 223-246.

Burleson, Clyde W., *Effective Meetings, The Complete Guide*, NY: John Wiley & Sons, 1990, pp.5-11.

Bushe, Gervase R. & Coetzer, Graeme H., "Group Development and Team Effectiveness," *The Journal of Applied Behavioral Science*, Vol. 43, No. 2 (June, 2007), pp. 184-212.

Chang, Richard Y. & Kehoe, Kevin R., *Meetings That Work*, CA: Richard Chang Associates, 1994, pp. 21-36.

Coghlin, David & Jacobs, Claus, "Kurt Lewin on Reeducation," *The Journal of Applied Behavioral Science*, Vol. 41, No. 4 (December, 2005), pp. 444-457.

Daniels, William R., Group Power I: *A Manager's Guide to Using Task-Force Meetings*, CA: University Associates, 1986, pp. 45-48.

Daniels, William R., *Group Power II: A Manager's Guide to Conducting Regular Meetings*, pp. 13-15.

Fisher, Roger, Ury, William, Patton, Bruce, *Getting to YES*, 2nd edition, NY: Penguin Books, 1991.

Fox, Robert S., et al, *Diagnosing Professional Climate of Schools*, VA: NTL Learning Resources Corp., Inc., 1973.

Goodlad, John, "Agenda for Education in a Democracy," (2008), Goodlad (May, 2010).

Janis, Irving L., "Groupthink," *Psychology Today*, (November, 1971), 5, pp. 43-46, 74-76. Taken from: Richard A Schmuck & Philip J. Runkel, *Handbook of Organizational Development in Schools*, Center for the Advanced Study of Educational Administration, University of Oregon, 1972, p. 292.

Katz, Daniel & Kahn, Robert, *The Social Psychology of Organizations*, NY: John Wiley & Sons, 1966, Taken from: Richard A Schmuck, Philip J. Runkel, The Second Handbook of Organizational Development in Schools, Center for the Advanced Study of Educational Administration, University of Oregon, CA: Mayfield Publishing Co., 1977, pp. 365-367.

Kelly, P. Keith, *Team Decision-Making Techniques*, CA: Richard Chang Associates, 1995, pp. 17-25.

Montebello, Anthony R., *Work Teams That Work*, MN: Best Sellers Publishing, pp. 102-112.

Maier, Norman, & Solem, Allen, *Human Relations*, 1952, 5, pp. 277-288. (17) Parker, Glenn & Hoffman, Robert, Meeting Excellence, CA: John Wiley & Sones, 2006, pp. 3-10, 28-31

Pokras, Sandy, *Team Problem Solving*, revised edition, CA: Crisp Publications, 1995.

Schein, Edgar H., *Organizational Psychology*, 3rd edition, NJ: Prentice- Hall Inc., 1980, pp. 169-170.

Schmuck, Richard A. & Runkel, Philip J., *Handbook of Organization Development in Schools*, University of Oregon, Center for the Advanced Study of Educational Administration, National Press Books, 1972, pp. 82-86.

Schmuck, Richard A. Runkel, Philip J, Arends, Jane H., Arends, Richard I., *The Second Handbook of Organization Development in Schools*, CA: Mayfield Publishing Co., 1977, pp. 91-92.

Schmuck, Richard A. & Runkel, Philip J., *Handbook of Organization Development in Schools*, 3rd edition, CA: Mayfield Publishing Co., 1985, pp. 387-88.

Senge, Peter M., *The Fifth Discipline*, revised, NY: Doubleday, 20006, pp. 222-232.

Silberman, Mel, *101 Ways to Make Meetings Active*, CA: Jossey-Bass Pfeiffer, 1999, pp. 21-23.

Stein, Judith, "Using the Stages of Team Development"

Tableman, Betty, "Parent Involvement in Schools," *BEST Practice Briefs*, No. 30-R, (June, 2004), University Outreach & Engagement at Michigan State University, Lansing, MI.

Ury, William. *Getting Past No; Negotiating with Difficult People*, NY: Bantam Books, 1991.*

Ury, William, Brett, Jeanne M., & Goldberg, Stephen B., *Getting Disputes Resolved, Designing Systems to Cut the Costs of Conflict*, CA: Jossey-Bass, Inc., 1988.*

*References denoted by an * are from the Negotiation Project at the Harvard Law School.*

Wageman, Ruth, Hackman, J. Richard, & Lehman, Erin, "Team Diagnostic Survey," *The Journal of Applied Behavioral Science*, Vol. 41, No. 4 (December, 2005), pp. 373-398.

Wallen, John, "The Interpersonal Gap," Oregon: Northwest Regional Educational Laboratory, 1972. From: Richard A. Schmuck & Philip J. Runkel, *Handbook of Organization Development in Schools*, University of Oregon, Center for the Advanced Study of Educational Administration, 1972, pp. 82-86.

Weaver, Richard G.. & Farrell, John D., *Managers as Facilitators*, CA: Berrett-Koehler Publishers, Inc., 1999, pp. 136-141.

Winwood, Richard I., *Creating Quality Meetings*, Utah: Franklin International Institute, Inc., 1991.

Worchel, Stephen, "Emphasizing the Social Nature of Groups in a Developmental Framework," *What's Social About Social Cognition?* edited by Judith L. Nye & Aaron M. Bower, CA: Sage Publications, 1996, pp. 261-282.

WEBSITES:

http://web.mit.edu/hr/oed/learn/teams/index.html
  • "How and Why to Use a Meeting Agenda"
  • "The Basics of Working on Teams"

www.michigan.gov/documents/Final_Parent_Involvement_Fact_Sheet_14732_7.pdf

www.nichcy.org/wp-content/uploads/docs/QA2.pdf

arksped.k12.ar.us/documents/policy/rulesandregulations/A4.pdf

My thanks to the following for critically reviewing earlier drafts of both books and providing thoughtful suggestions: Craig Barringer, Phil Eller, Lyn Haas, Nina McCampbell, Windham Northeast Special Education Compliance Improvement Team, & Joanne Scobie.

I also thank Jean Stone for editing my manuscript, Douglas Lufkin of Lufkin Graphic Designs for making it look great, and Linda Roghaar of White River Press for publishing my books.

The information contained herein follows federal guidelines for special education. Please refer to your individual state to be certain all information is correct for and appropriate to your state.

CPSIA information can be obtained
at www.ICGtesting.com
Printed in the USA
BVHW081930300620
582602BV00002B/180